Will War
Ever End?

Will War Ever End?

A Soldier's

Vision of Peace

for the 21st Century

Captain Paul K. Chappell,
U.S. Army

Ashoka Books
2009

Published by:
Ashoka Books
An imprint of Rvive Books
8 Gray's Farm Road
Weston, Connecticut 06883
www.rvive.com

Distributed by Ingram Publisher Services

ISBN: 978-1935073024

DISCLAIMER
The views presented here do not necessarily represent
the views of the Department of Defense or its components,
or the United States Government.

www.paulkchappell.com

Printed in the United States of America

Printed on recycled paper and paper manufactured
using sustainable production methods.

First Printing: February 2009

10 9 8 7 6 5 4 3 2 1

For my parents,
the brave soldiers I have served with,
and
all who have suffered because of war.

ACKNOWLEDGMENTS

I would like to thank my agent, Bill Gladstone, for taking a chance on a young new author, always having faith in this project, and being a loyal friend during difficult times. I would also like to thank Ming Russell and Nathalie McKnight at Waterside Productions for encouraging and supporting me throughout the publishing process. I would like to thank Susan McCombs for pulling one of my manuscripts out of a slush pile several years ago and becoming interested in my writing; and I must thank Patricia Heinicke for taking the time to hone and refine my skills as a writer. I owe so much to my editor and good friend, Vicki Weiland, whose talent and dedication greatly improved this manuscript and whose generous help continues to inspire me. I am extremely grateful to David Wilk for enthusiastically believing in this message, agreeing to publish this book, and being a comrade in the struggle for a brighter future. I am also indebted to Gray Cutler for skillfully copyediting the manuscript, Barbara Aronica-Buck for beautifully designing the book, and Dave Grossman for writing the foreword and influencing my ideas with his groundbreaking research, brilliant insights into the problem of violence, and bold determination to make our world more peaceful. Finally, I must thank Jo Ann Deck. Words cannot express how important she has been in helping me bring this hopeful message to the world. She is the best friend anyone could ask for and the person who made all of this possible.

Lt. Col. Dave Grossman, U.S. Army (ret.)
author of
On Killing: The Psychological Cost of
Learning to Kill in War and Society

The book you hold in your hand makes a powerful new contribution to our understanding of war and peace, and provides us with vital insights into fundamental aspects of human nature. I sincerely believe that the fields of philosophy, anthropology, history, military science, peace studies, and many others, will be able to build upon the concepts set forth in this book in order to help guide our civilization toward a world without war.

A bold statement? Perhaps. Read this book and see what you think.

As for me, I was consumed with an admiration verging on awe when I first read this book. Paul K. Chappell's concepts of fury, rage, and "the pain of hatred" struck me with an almost physical impact. He has transformed my way of thinking about war and peace. And I believe (and hope, and pray) that his powerful logic and lucid insights will continue to contribute to our civilization for generations to come.

My book, *On Killing: The Psychological Cost of Learning to Kill in War and Society*, is currently being used as "required reading" in peace studies programs at Berkeley, and in Mennonite and Quaker colleges.

On Killing is also on the U.S. Marine Corps Commandant's "Required Reading List" and is required reading at the FBI Academy and in courses at West Point. How do you make institutions as diverse as Berkeley, the FBI, the Quakers, the U.S. Army and the Marine Corps happy with the same book? The answer is: you just tell the truth. New truths. Powerful truths. Useful truths.

I freely and willingly take whatever credibility *On Killing* gives me, and "put it on the line" to commend this book to your attention. For it has provided me with new, powerful, and useful truths. This book has drawn from my work (and that of many others, for mine is but a small contribution) and brought them to a deeper, more useful, and more important level.

And there is cause to hope, and believe, that there can be an end to war.

The West has won the Cold War without resorting to mega-death, genocide, or nuclear holocaust. For the first time in history the majority of the world's population elects their national leaders, and democratically elected governments generally do not go to war with other democracies.

Writing in his syndicated newspaper column, political science professor Bradley R. Gitz flatly states "there is no agreed-upon historical case of a democratically elected government going to war against another democratically elected government." He believes that one of the "axioms" of political science is that "democratic states don't fight democratic states or provide support for terrorist groups." He quotes political scientist John Mueller, who "has gone so far as to assert that war between such states has become 'subrationally unthinkable,' not even on the radar screen of options to be considered as a means of resolving disputes."

With the Soviet Union and the Warsaw pact gone, the goal of democracies around the world is to foster democracy. Once a nation has become a democracy, it has effectively been "inoculated" against going to war with other democracies.

Thus, there is, in our time, cause to hope for an end to war. And we didn't just get here overnight. If we look for it, we can observe a persistent trend toward "limiting" war. We can see it with the classical Greeks, who for four centuries refused to implement use of the bow and arrow even after being introduced to it in a most unpleasant way by Persian archers.

In *Giving Up the Gun*, Noel Perrin tells how the Japanese banned firearms after their introduction by the Portuguese in the 1500s. The Japanese quickly recognized that the military use of gunpowder threatened their society and culture. Thus they moved aggressively to defend their way of life. The feuding Japanese warlords destroyed all existing firearms and made the production or import of any new guns punishable by death. Three centuries later, when Commodore Perry forced the Japanese to open their ports, they did not even have the technology to make firearms. Similarly, the Chinese invented gunpowder but elected not to use it in warfare.

The most encouraging examples of restraining killing technology have all occurred in the twentieth century. After the tragic experience of using poisonous gases in World War I the world has generally rejected their use ever since. The atmospheric nuclear test ban treaty and the ban on the deployment of anti-satellite weapons are both still going strong across many turbulent decades, and the United States and the former USSR have been steadily reducing their stockpiles of nuclear weapons since the end of the Cold War.

Heckler points out that there has been "an almost unnoticed series of precedents for reducing military technology on moral grounds," precedents that show the way for understanding that we do have a choice about how we think about war, about killing, and about the value of human life in our society.

In recent years we have exercised the choice to step back from the brink of nuclear destruction. We have moved the world toward democratically elected states that are "inoculated" against going to war with each other. There is, indeed, good cause to hope for an end to war. And I believe, with all my heart, that in this book Paul K. Chappell has made a major contribution toward that most worthy and noble endeavor.

Lt. Col. Dave Grossman, U.S. Army (ret.) has served as an Airborne Ranger infantry officer and West Point psychology professor, and is the Director of the Warrior Science Group. He is the author or co-author of several books, including *On Killing*, which was nominated for the Pulitzer Prize.

A Manifesto for Waging Peace

As fire does not extinguish fire, so evil cannot extinguish evil. Only goodness, meeting evil and not infected by it, conquers evil. That this is so is in man's spiritual world an immutable law comparable to the law of Galileo.

—Leo Tolstoy [1]

The Soldier above all other people prays for peace,
for he must suffer and bear the deepest wounds
and scars of war.
—General Douglas MacArthur[2]

Since my earliest memories, I have been obsessed with war. My father served in the Korean and Vietnam wars, and when I was young I saw how war can ruin families. I grew up as an only child in Alabama, and I have fond memories of being three years old and watching my father tend to his garden, feed the birds in our backyard, and chase away a spider that almost frightened me to death. But when I was four years old, everything changed.

I was sleeping peacefully late one night when I felt someone grab my leg and drag me from my bed onto the floor. This person pulled my leg so hard that I heard my pajama pants rip down the middle. Looking up and seeing my father, I began to panic as he pulled my hair and told me he was going to kill me. His cursing and my screaming woke my mother, who ran into the room and bear-hugged him until he finally calmed down.

When I was four years old, something else

occurred that I could not understand at the time, but that I would later attribute to my father's experiences during war. One evening, I heard my father screaming at my mother as he threatened to shoot himself with his pistol. This was the first time I heard him threaten to commit suicide, but it would not be the last. Throughout my childhood, I watched my father lose his grip on reality, and his frightening behavior caused me to struggle with my own sanity. Rage overshadowed his once peaceful nature, and when I heard him complain about violent nightmares, I realized that something called war had taken my gentle father from me.

During these years, I internalized my father's despair and longed for an escape from his violent behavior. When I was five, this trauma led to my lifelong obsession with suffering and war—when I had a vivid dream that I killed myself. I still remember the dream clearly: I walked through the front door of my house, where I saw both my parents lying dead in coffins. Without thinking, I went to the bathroom cabinet with the intent of stabbing myself in the heart. I opened a drawer and saw a large pair of scissors, but their menacing size frightened me. Next to them, I saw a smaller pair of scissors that my mother used to clip my fingernails. I picked them up, stabbed myself in the chest, and watched as blood covered my hands. Then I walked to my mother's coffin and laid in it with her, where I waited to die so that my anguish would finally end.

Ever since I woke up from that dream, I have been obsessed with learning if and how war could ever end. Seeing how war had affected my parents fueled this obsession throughout my childhood. Growing up during the Great Depression in Virginia, my father was half white and half black, and he joined the army when it was still segregated. My father was a career soldier who spent thirty years in the military, was decorated for valor during combat, and retired at the highest enlisted rank. My mother was not a stranger to war either. Born in Japan, she experienced war as a small girl during World War II. Her family later moved to Korea, where she lived during the Korean War.

When I was a teenager, I wanted to know if war will ever end. But I realized that I could never know the answer to this question unless I also asked and answered some fundamental questions about human nature. Are human beings naturally violent? Throughout world history, why does war seem like the norm and why does peace seem like the anomaly? Is war an inescapable part of human nature? When I was in eighth grade I asked one my teachers, "Where does war come from?" "Human beings are naturally violent and warlike," she told me. "War is a part of human nature, because people are evil. It is human nature to be greedy, hateful, and selfish." As I pondered her response to my question, I realized that her answer did not make sense. If human beings are naturally violent and warlike, why does war drive so many people like my father insane?

From that point onward, I was determined to study war the way a doctor studies an illness. Only then could I understand if world peace would ever become more than a cliché. By studying war, I hoped to learn if General Douglas MacArthur was correct when he said, "Only the dead have seen the end of war."[3] I also hoped to learn if war is truly an inescapable part of human nature or if it is even possible to define human nature. I did not know where these questions would take me, but I did know that if war and violence were truly a part of human nature, it would be naïve to assume war would ever end. As I explored the causes and cure for war, however, I began to find strong evidence which showed that people are not naturally violent.

When I attended West Point in 1998 as a freshman, I read a book called *On Killing: The Psychological Cost of Learning to Kill in War and Society*. This book was written by Dave Grossman, a lieutenant colonel in the army and a former West Point psychology professor. In *On Killing* Grossman said, "War is an environment that will psychologically debilitate 98 percent of all who participate in it for any length of time. And the 2 percent who are not driven insane by war appear to have already been insane—aggressive psychopaths—before coming to the battlefield."[4] These words conveyed a fact about war I already knew from witnessing my father's agony, but Grossman expressed other profound ideas that changed how I saw war, along with the potential for peace.

In *On Killing* Grossman said that human beings have an innate resistance to killing other human beings. A country is only capable of waging war, he explained, if propaganda is used to dehumanize the enemy. Sometimes this dehumanization process consists of calling the enemy derogatory names such as "Krauts," "Japs," or "Gooks." In other instances it consists of stereotyping the enemy as the epitome of everything evil in the world while believing that one's own country is the source of everything good, moral, or holy.

The only way to kill human beings and not experience guilt or remorse is to imagine they are not human beings. This involves viewing people as subhuman—so we can rationalize the act of killing—or seeing people as evil monsters so we can perceive the act of killing as a necessary purging of evil from the world. Grossman also explains that the most traumatic experiences in war occur when someone kills a human being, not when someone is in physical danger. According to Grossman's extensive research, the survivors of the London bombings during World War II did not suffer as much psychological trauma as the soldiers in Vietnam who killed men, women, and children at close range, where they could see the faces of their victims.

Every Army's Greatest Problem

When I studied the evidence that shows human beings have an innate resistance to killing, I became more determined to answer my second question: why does war seem like the norm and peace seem like the anomaly throughout human history? As I studied military history at West Point, I realized there is a deeper and more intriguing story to the history of warfare, and that everything is not as it first appears. Although war is common throughout history, the greatest problem of every army has been this: when a battle begins, how do you stop soldiers from running away? Where our fight-or-flight response is concerned, the vast majority of people prefer to run when a sword is wielded against them, a spear is thrust in their direction, a bullet flies over their head, or a bomb explodes in their vicinity. In the U.S. Army, a complex system of conditioning trains soldiers to stay and fight—but the ancient Greeks discovered a more effective method still used today.

The Greeks understood that it is not easy to make soldiers stay and fight during a battle. Human beings are not naturally violent after all, because if we were, the majority of people would not be terrified of violence when they experience it up close and personal. If human beings were naturally violent, our "fight response" would be far more powerful than our "flight response," but in fact the opposite is true. Getting soldiers to run away and retreat during a battle is easy. Getting them to stand their ground, fight, and kill other human beings is the challenge.

The Greeks realized, however, that one simple thing could give soldiers endless courage when their lives were threatened and convince them to not only stay and fight, but to sacrifice their lives. At first glance the Greeks' solution might seem like a contradiction, because the most powerful motivator that convinces people to stay and fight is not a natural propensity for violence or killing, but their capacity for love and compassion. Halfway around the world, Lao-tzu, a Chinese philosopher who lived during the sixth century BC, also acknowledged this fundamental truth about human nature when he said, "By being loving, we are capable of being brave."[5] Because the ancient Greeks discovered this fact about human nature, they were able to protect their homeland from Persian conquest during the fifth century BC.

In 490 BC, during the Battle of Marathon, the

Persians landed on the Greek shore in an attempt to conquer Greece. By some estimates the Athenian soldiers were outnumbered ten to one. Despite the numerical superiority of the Persian military, the Athenians repelled the invading force and saved their country from destruction. Ten years later in 480 BC, the Persians again tried to conquer Greece. During the Battle of Salamis, the Athenian navy was greatly outnumbered by the Persian fleet, but the Athenians again refused to retreat and were victorious once more.

To inspire the courage that made this victory possible, the Athenian warriors shouted the battle cry "Advance, ye sons of Greece. From oppression save your country, save your wives, save your children . . . This day, the common cause of all demands your valor." Although they were greatly outnumbered, the Athenians refused to retreat because they were fighting to protect the lives of their loved ones.

I find it odd that people refer to compassion and love as naïve moral ideals that make one weak, while the U.S. Army uses compassion and love to motivate its soldiers to cooperate and survive in the harshest circumstances. In the army I was taught to treat my military unit like my family and to fight in order to "protect the person to my left and to my right." At West Point I learned a famous passage from Shakespeare's *Henry V* that reads: "We few, we happy few, we band of brothers; for he today that sheds his blood with me shall be my brother . . ." This ideal of love and brotherhood is responsible for most acts of heroism, along with many of the Medal of Honor recipients who sacrificed themselves to save the lives of their friends. We can see the power of compassion in people such as Private First Class Frederick C. Murphy, who served as a medic during World War II. His citation for the Medal of Honor reads:

> An aid man, he was wounded in the right shoulder soon after his comrades had jumped off in a dawn attack 18 March 1945, against the Siegfried Line at Saarlautern, Germany. He refused to withdraw for treatment and continued forward, administering first aid under heavy machine gun, mortar, and artillery fire. When the company ran into a thickly sown antipersonnel minefield and began to suffer more and more casualties, he continued to disregard his own wound and unhesitatingly braved the danger of exploding mines, moving about through heavy fire and helping the injured until he stepped on a mine which severed one of his feet. In spite of his grievous wounds, he struggled on with his work, refusing to be evacuated and crawling from man to man administering to them while in great pain and bleeding profusely. He was killed by the blast of another mine which he had dragged himself across in an

effort to reach still another casualty. With in-domitable courage, and unquenchable spirit of self-sacrifice and supreme devotion to duty which made it possible for him to continue performing his tasks while barely able to move, Pfc. Murphy saved many of his fellow soldiers at the cost of his own life.[7]

The Medal of Honor is the highest award a soldier can receive, but when I studied the Medal of Honor recipients while I was at West Point, I realized something surprising. If human beings are naturally violent, as some suggest, then the highest military award should be given for the act of killing, and the person who kills the most people should receive the highest award. However, many of the Medal of Honor recipients I studied never killed a single person. Why then do so many people assume that we are naturally violent, I wondered, if the highest military award is given to those who display incredible selflessness and compassion on the battlefield? And how can compassion not be a defining characteristic of human nature, I thought, if the most admired trait in soldiers is not their ability to kill, but their willingness to sacrifice for their friends?

THE KEY TO HUMAN SURVIVAL

Before I could answer these questions and discover whether human beings are naturally peaceful or violent, I had to ask and answer a more fundamental question: why does compassion encourage these acts of heroism? As I explored the reality of human nature, I realized that compassion's influence on the battlefield is not a contradiction, but one of the reasons why our ancestors were able to survive in the harshest conditions. And why we, their descendents, are capable of ending war.

Our earliest human ancestors lived on the plains of Africa, but when I was a teenager, I often wondered how they could have possibly survived. After all, human beings are not very fast. We are much slower than lions, leopards, and other predators, and we lack natural weapons such as fangs, claws, tusks, and horns. We are physically weaker than chimpanzees and gorillas, and we lack the climbing agility that allows them to quickly escape to the safety of trees. With such significant drawbacks, how did human beings survive and prosper in the harsh conditions of Africa?

We survived because of our large brains and our endless capacity to cooperate. In fact, our large brains make us even more dependent upon cooperation, because our intelligence cannot develop unless a community protects us and gives us the gifts of language and knowledge while we are young. Because our large brains take many years to fully mature, a human child remains helpless for a longer period of time than the offspring of any organism and requires a community to further its growth and development.

All mammals cooperate to some degree, while many mammals rely on cooperation for their survival. Lions live in prides, for example, while elephants live in herds, wolves in packs, dolphins in pods, and chimpanzees in troops. But due to our physical limitations, along with the conditions our large brains require to fully develop, we rely on cooperation far more than any other mammal.

Many people do not understand that cooperation is the key to our survival, because they incorrectly assume that the purpose of every organism is merely to survive, reproduce, or provide for its self-interest, but this is not true. In a hive of honeybees, only the queen bee is capable of reproduction. The female worker bee labors for the well-being of her community, and in an act of ultimate self-sacrifice, every worker bee must give her life when she defends her hive, by leaving behind her vital organs when she delivers her defensive sting.

Where mammals are concerned, a gorilla will die to protect its family members and a wolf will die to defend its pack. Gorillas, wolves, and other mammals serve their community because the purpose of every organism is not merely to survive, reproduce, or provide for its self-interest, but to continue the survival of its species. Because bees, ants, gorillas, and wolves rely upon their communities for survival, they are instinctually willing to protect their communities at the risk of losing their lives.

THE INDESTRUCTIBLE BOND

Since human beings, more than all other mammals, require cooperation to survive, our reliance upon our community is even more important for us. To survive, we have a bond powerful enough to hold a community together and to encourage selfless service, sacrifice, and cooperation among its members. If you and I were stranded in the wilderness, my genuine concern for your well-being would be the only bond strong enough to prevent me from leaving you when times were hard, killing you when food was scarce, or breaking the cooperation that allowed us both to survive. This is why our genuine concern for the well-being of others, also known as unconditional love, is not a naïve moral virtue but a crucial survival instinct that makes cooperation possible.

My experiences in the military allowed me to

understand this fact about unconditional love. If a soldier's friend or loved one is in danger, the soldier will often risk his or her life to protect that friend or loved one. This is an instinctual response that occurs when we see those we care about in danger, because on the dangerous plains of Africa our ancestors were not fast enough to run away from a pride of hungry lions. They had to stand their ground and frighten these predators away by brandishing torches, wielding large sticks, throwing rocks, and so on.

In the military, this bond of love and brotherhood among soldiers is absolutely necessary for their survival. One afternoon while I was deployed in Baghdad, I heard an explosion in the distance while I was on my way to lunch. In Iraq such noise was common, so I paid little attention and continued walking. I had taken only a few steps when I heard something approaching from behind me. At first it sounded like a jet, but it was flying too low. Something was wrong, I realized, as the noise roared closer. Before I could turn around I heard something pass over my head. A split second later a deafening explosion shook the earth. Seventy-five meters in front of me, a 157-millimeter Katyusha rocket had slammed into the army base where I and many other soldiers worked. Since these rocket attacks came in groups, I immediately took cover and heard several more blasts. Within a minute, the attack was over and a momentary silence ensued, followed by screams.

I ran to check on the wounded, smelling smoke and blood as I neared the point of impact. Several vehicles were on fire, and a crowd of soldiers had already gathered around the injured to offer them medical treatment and words of comfort. Over a dozen people were hurt during this mass attack, but dozens more had come to their rescue. The suffering of their comrades had called them to action without hesitation, summoning them to help and to heal. In this chaos I witnessed a power that all people have. This is the same strength that calls people to action when they hear the cries of their loved ones. This is the same bond that exists between parents and children or any members of a close family.

Unconditional love builds an indestructible bond between people, because it encourages us to care about the well-being of others with no concern for what we will receive in return. The plains of Africa were so dangerous for our earliest human ancestors that this indestructible bond was necessary to keep communities together despite the harshest circumstances. This indestructible bond is just as crucial for the survival of communities today, because it allows us to help each other and remain united as a team when overcoming any significant obstacle.

WHY BEARS ROAR

If we look at military history again, we will realize that unconditional love and compassion encourage people to stand their ground and protect their loved ones during a battle, but not to kill. Human beings are not naturally violent, because when people with no military training are placed in dangerous situations such as combat, their flight response is much stronger than their fight response, which would urge them to kill. However, even people with no military training find that their flight response is weak in comparison to their instinct to protect their loved ones. If you saw an animal attacking your child, spouse, or close friend, you would not require any military training to rush to their aid. This is because our instinct to protect our loved ones is the strongest instinct in a human being. It is even more powerful than our instinct for self-preservation.

When we must protect our loved ones or ourselves we do not rely upon a fight response that urges us to kill, but a "frighten response" that encourages us to chase away potential threats so that we do not have to kill or risk being injured. In *On Killing* Dave Grossman explains that human beings have a stronger instinct to frighten their enemies away (an act he calls posturing) than to kill.

Posturing can be seen in the plumed helmets of the ancient Greeks and Romans, which allowed the bearer to appear taller and therefore fiercer to his foe, while the brilliantly shined armor made him seem broader and brighter. Such plumage saw its height in modern history during the Napoleonic era, when soldiers wore bright uniforms and high, uncomfortable shako hats, which served no other purpose than to make the wearer look and feel like a taller, more dangerous creature. In the same manner, the roars of two posturing beasts are exhibited by men in battle. For centuries the war cries of soldiers have made their opponents' blood run cold. Whether it be the battle cry of the Greek phalanx, the "hurrah!" of the Russian infantry, the wail of Scottish bagpipes, or the Rebel yell of our own Civil War, soldiers have always instinctively sought to daunt the enemy through nonviolent means prior to physical conflict, while encouraging one another and impressing themselves with their own ferocity and simultaneously providing a very effective means of drowning the disagreeable yell of the enemy.[8]

Our preference for posturing over killing even led to the use of gunpowder. Although the longbow was a much deadlier weapon, armies preferred the smoothbore musket because it made a louder noise when fired. Grossman explains:

> Gunpowder's superior *noise*, its superior *posturing* ability, made it ascendant on the battlefield. The longbow would still have been used in the Napoleonic Wars if the raw mathematics of killing effectiveness was all that mattered, since both the longbow's firing rate and its accuracy were *much* greater than that of a smoothbore musket. But a frightened man, thinking with his midbrain and going "ploink, ploink, ploink" with a bow, doesn't stand a chance against an equally frightened man going "BANG! BANG!" with a musket. Firing a musket or rifle clearly fills the deep-seated need to posture, and it even meets the requirements of being relatively harmless when we consider the consistent historical occurrences of firing over the enemy's head, and the remarkable ineffectiveness of such fire.[9]

In the same way that dogs growl when they feel threatened, rattlesnakes shake their tails, bears roar, and gorillas beat their chests, our instincts urge us to frighten away potential predators through the act of posturing. For this reason posturing is a crucial survival instinct in human beings and many other mammals. If a bear is confronted by several wolves, for example, scaring these wolves away is more effective than fighting. Even if this larger animal is able to kill the wolves, the bear might break its leg during this fight, get bitten and die from infection, or suffer another life-threatening injury.

When confronted by hungry lions, our earliest ancestors would have been safer if they threw rocks, brandished torches and spears, and used formations and noise to frighten these predators away. Although our earliest ancestors could have used their tactics and tools to kill a group of hungry lions, avoiding the fight altogether was preferable to a dangerous battle that might have led to human casualties. When a person was severely wounded thousands of years ago, they could not be rushed to an emergency room. They would have died a slow, painful death.

Not All Soldiers Are Human Beings

As Grossman explains, posturing is an instinctual behavior that armies have exhibited throughout history. Every army has demonstrated some form of posturing, even though many soldiers never understood why they were compelled to behave in this manner. Instinctually, they simply felt the need to yell and make noise during a battle to frighten their enemies away, just as a bear will roar when confronted by other predators. Instinctually, soldiers also felt a need to make themselves appear taller, larger, and more dangerous to their foe, just as a cobra will lift its body and spread its hood to ward off anything it perceives as a threat. Because this instinctual behavior is deeply ingrained in our unconscious mind, posturing is a nonviolent response to danger that transcends national and cultural boundaries.

Since unconditional love is also deeply ingrained in our unconscious mind, it also transcends national and cultural boundaries. How do we know that unconditional love is instinctual and peaceful behavior is a defining characteristic of what it means to be a human being? As we have seen, the Greeks understood that love encourages soldiers to protect their friends and family, while halfway around the world Lao-tzu realized that being loving allows us to be brave. In the U.S. Army, as in ancient Greece, the most admired trait in soldiers is not their ability to kill but their willingness to sacrifice for their friends.

The Battle of Thermopylae occurred in Greece in 480 BC, when three hundred Spartan soldiers and their allies held off an invading Persian army. Since then, more people throughout the world have looked to this battle for inspiration than perhaps any other battle in history. I always found this interesting, since the Battle of Thermopylae did not inspire countless generations of people because the Spartans won, but because they lost. The Spartans at Thermopylae are admired because they stood courageously against overwhelming odds and died to protect their loved ones. These are the same reasons why many Medal of Honor recipients are admired today.

Although we could list countless examples of unconditional love from every era in history, I cannot say that every mammal shares the experience we call unconditional love, because I can only speak from my own experiences as a human being. However, I can show that other mammals are willing to protect and sacrifice for the members of their group, even if they are not related to these members by blood. Whether we call this behavior unconditional love or not, abundant evidence reveals that dogs, wolves, and primates exhibit selfless behavior that contributes to the well-being of others.

Many of the soldiers who served as dog handlers during the Vietnam War, for example, would certainly agree that dogs are capable of experiencing unconditional love, and these soldiers have a lot of evidence to support this claim. There is a reason, after all, why human beings have forged such a strong bond with dogs, and why dogs are considered man's best friend. Because of its pack mentality, a dog can become a valued member of a human family. The army takes humanity's close kinship with dogs even further.

In the army today dogs are not viewed as pieces of equipment, but as soldiers. In fact, military working dogs are given rank, promotions, and awards just like human soldiers, and they always outrank their dog handlers. When army dogs complete their military service, they even receive a retirement ceremony along with an honorable discharge before they are given to a civilian family for adoption. Although the behavior of dogs differs from that of human beings in many ways, military working dogs reveal that we share one form of behavior crucial to our survival. The following example will better explain why many people in the army do not see dogs as pieces of equipment, but as soldiers who are capable of expressing unconditional love.

During the Vietnam War, the most dangerous position for a soldier on patrol was walking "point." Because the soldier marched in front of the patrol, he would be the first person attacked by the enemy during an ambush and the most likely person to die from a booby trap. Due to these dangers, the soldier walking point was often a dog handler. Military working dogs were trained to smell enemy ambushes, locate snipers, and could even hear trip wires vibrating in the breeze.

In 1969, Corporal John Flannelly served as a dog handler in Vietnam with a German shepherd named Bruiser. "They had told us that this dog was going to be my new best friend," he said, "and that I would probably get closer to him than any human being that

I have ever known in my entire life, and they were right. I was closer with that dog than most people are with their wives, their children . . . we were inseparable."

In September of 1969, Flannelly and Bruiser were leading their platoon on a patrol through enemy territory when Bruiser spotted danger. "All of a sudden Bruiser stopped dead in his tracks. His nose was up and his ears were twitching, and I noticed some movement from the bush. I had to make a decision, and I chose to fire. The next thing I knew, all hell broke loose. There were automatic weapons fired, hand grenades, rockets being fired."

An explosion tore Flannelly's body apart and knocked him to the ground. "I looked down. I thought my arm was blown off. My whole side was blown open. I could actually watch my left lung filling up and down, and then I watched it slowly deflate. Bruiser was just standing next to me, looking at me. He had a very sad look in his eyes. He knew we were in way over our heads. I didn't want him to be there. I didn't want him to have to see me die. I told him, 'Bruiser . . . go . . . go.' It was very hard, because every time I spoke I was just spitting up blood, and I was just trying to stay conscious, because I just wanted to get him out of there before I died. He wouldn't leave."

Instead of leaving, Bruiser tugged on Flannelly's uniform with his teeth. Realizing that Bruiser was trying to pull him to safety, Flannelly grabbed on to Bruiser's body harness with his good arm. Bruiser then dragged Flannelly away from the gunfire and explosions. "He dragged me back. I'm not sure how far it was. It seemed like forever. I don't know where he got the strength to pull me. While he was dragging me, he was hit I believe two times, but he was determined to get me out of there. His loyalty was immeasurable. I'll never be able to thank him enough for that. I owe my life to that dog."[10]

Other mammals display incredible acts of selflessness, but since human beings must rely on cooperation far more than any other mammal to survive, we have a unique human ability that makes us different from every other mammal. Because we can strengthen our unconditional love to a limitless degree, we have the capacity for universal love, which is the ability to love all of humanity, even all life. Two of the most admired and influential people in history—Jesus and Gautama Buddha—embraced our unique human capacity for universal love. Martin Luther King Jr., Mahatma Gandhi, Albert Schweitzer, Mother Teresa, and Henry David Thoreau also demonstrated that human beings have an endless capacity for unconditional love. To understand how our endless capacity for unconditional love gives us our endless capacity to cooperate and survive, we must further explore how unconditional love gives us the power to end war.

FURY AND RAGE

Because we rely upon cooperation to survive, we have a strong inclination to live peacefully with each other and a powerful instinct to protect our loved ones. When we see our loved ones in danger and our unconditional love fuses with adrenaline, this leads to the behavior I call fury. I use the word *fury* because, as far as I know, these selfless actions that seek to protect our loved ones have never been fully defined, explained, or given a name until now. Fury is a survival instinct that makes us natural protectors, but not natural killers, since our fury is satisfied when hostilities end and our loved ones are safe. For this reason, fury transcends the battlefield by encouraging selfless action during any life-and-death situation.

In 1987, a Buddhist monk named Jampa Tenzin demonstrated fury during a peaceful protest against Chinese rule in Tibet. During this nonviolent march, the Chinese police began shooting at the civilian protestors. When a police station caught on fire, the police officers took the Buddhist monks they had arrested into a back room and began executing them. Hearing the gunshots, Jampa Tenzin ran into the burning station and through the first several rooms, which were collapsing. He helped rescue the remaining monks, who safely escaped. Surrounded by onlookers, Jampa Tenzin emerged with his body severely burned, his skin charred. Raising his hand in solidarity, he was hoisted onto the shoulders of the marchers. Passing in and out of consciousness from the pain of his wounds, he became a symbol of inspiration as the protest continued.[11]

Jampa Tenzin showed that fury can overcome any danger, while the following example helped me better understand how fury seeks to stop rather than escalate violence. One of my training partners in mixed martial arts was out with his friend one evening, when his friend was attacked by a stranger. My training partner did not want to hurt the attacker; he just wanted to stop the fight. Using a wrestling takedown, my training partner forced the stranger to the ground and made him surrender by using a submission hold. When his concern for the well-being of his friend fused with adrenaline, my training partner experienced fury, which was focused upon stopping the fight. When hatred fuses with adrenaline, however, rage is produced. Unlike fury, rage does not seek to stop a fight and end hostilities, but to escalate the violence. Rage is less concerned with protecting the person being harmed and more focused upon hurting the person committing the offense. If my training partner had been motivated by rage instead of fury, he would have probably killed the stranger.

In a small tribe or family, people may sometimes fight each other. When this occurs, fury that strives to "stop the fight" is more conducive to our survival than rage which seeks to escalate violence. Rage threatens our community by causing us to lose control and go berserk, but fury empowers us to protect our community by taking action. Although the Greeks instilled fury in their soldiers so they would not retreat, fury alone cannot transform an army into an aggressive killing machine. Athenians such as Aristotle believed Greeks were the master race and all non-Greeks were barbarians. Consequently, many ancient Athenians viewed all non-Greeks as subhuman. This notion of racial superiority that dehumanizes the enemy leads to hatred, and when hatred fuses with adrenaline, rage is produced.

But how can we be certain that fury promotes human survival and rage endangers it? How can we know that unconditional love is a defining part of human nature that always benefits our community, and that hatred occurs when we ignore our true nature? How can we prove that unconditional love makes us psychologically healthy and that hatred, just like an illness, occurs when something has gone wrong? To explain this we must explore the nature of hatred.

THE BURN OF HATRED

If human beings were naturally violent and destructive, hatred would not hurt every single time, with no exceptions. We know that hatred always hurts, because if hatred felt good, then men in the Ku Klux Klan would marry African American women, adopt African American children, and join African American churches so they could be around the object of their hatred all the time. But this is an absurd notion. Hatred is so painful that in small doses it causes us to remove the object of hatred from sight and in large doses urges us to destroy it.

If we look deeper, however, we will realize that the pain of hatred does not derive from any object or person, but from our hatred itself. Hatred hurts for the same reason that placing your hand in a fire hurts. When you place your hand in a fire, a painful burning sensation will warn that you are endangering your body. When you harbor destructive thoughts toward the members of your community, the painful burn of hatred will warn that you are endangering the body of your human family, upon which your survival depends.

Hatred sometimes leads to murder because the causes of psychological pain are not as obvious as the causes of physical pain, such as burning your hand, stepping on a nail, or being bitten by an animal. I can easily see that a fire is burning my hand and remove it from the fire, but unlike a fire, thoughts and emotions are invisible. If my hand was being burned by an invisible fire, I might wrongly assume that my hand was causing my pain and foolishly proceed to cut off my limb. In this same way, Ku Klux Klansmen wrongly assume that African Americans (a limb of their human community), rather than their burning destructive thoughts, are the source of their suffering. When they proceed to kill African Americans, they have misidentified the source of their suffering, which causes them to cut off a limb from their human community.

When people suggest that hatred can produce pleasure, they forget that pleasure is relative. Here is an example that better explains this. If I have been getting punched in the face every moment of every day for the past ten years, then getting punched in the arm will feel less painful. Although getting punched in the arm still hurts, I might mistake this decrease in pain for pleasure. Similarly, if someone is depressed and has no reason to live, the burn of hatred might feel better than a meaningless life. Although hatred still hurts, just as getting punched in the arm still hurts, hatred can seem less painful than a purposeless life, just as getting punched in the arm can seem less painful than getting punched in the face. The pleasure of hatred is based on a relative pleasure, or decrease in pain, rather than an increase in genuine happiness.

Neo-Nazi groups in America today commonly recruit young people with low self-esteem and a weak sense of identity. To youths with no meaning or purpose in life, a message of hatred may sound appealing and uplifting because it takes them from getting punched in the face to getting punched in the arm. They go from having no reason to live, to the burn of hatred that gives them meaning through destruction.

History teaches us that hatred is one cause of war, but to understand why these people suffer from hatred, we can compare hatred to a preventable illness. Physical health promotes our survival, but this does not mean everyone in the world is healthy. Similarly, unconditional love promotes our survival, but this does not mean everyone is compassionate, loving, and courageous. Hatred, like an illness, occurs when something has gone wrong, when we have strayed from our highest potential, but unlike all other illnesses, every person has the power to forever cure their hatred.

Since human beings and their predecessors lived in small tribes for millions of years on the harsh plains of Africa, harboring destructive thoughts toward the members of their small communities would have led to self-destruction. Because hatred endangers the survival of our community, hatred always hurts. On the other hand, unconditional love is an inherently joyful feeling because unconditional love allows us to perceive others as friends, family, and loved ones.

By improving our outlook on the world, unconditional love gives us an internal source of happiness based on our attitude toward the grandeur of life. Unconditional love gives us this potent form of happiness while also promoting our survival. This is not a coincidence, since the profound joy of unconditional love is a way to encourage the behavior that allows us to survive.

Unconditional Love Is Stronger Than Hatred

When I studied philosophy, the major world religions, and the people who made our planet a better place to live, it reinforced my understanding that human beings are not naturally violent. Buddhism, Christianity, Judaism, and Hinduism all express the idea that caring about others gives us our highest form of happiness, and that unconditional love is stronger than hatred. Humanity's greatest visionaries agree that when someone embraces unconditional love, that person will not only experience a fulfilling and meaningful life, but will gain the strength to improve the well-being of his community. History teaches us that an abundance of hatred can drive a human being insane, while an abundance of unconditional love leads to a joyful life and creates people such as Martin Luther King Jr., Mahatma Gandhi, and Albert Schweitzer.

As was the case with Adolf Hitler and Joseph Stalin, anyone filled with hatred is extremely dangerous to human survival. Because of Hitler and Stalin, tens of millions of people died. On the other hand, when you place someone such as Martin Luther King Jr., Mahatma Gandhi, or Albert Schweitzer in any community, whether local or global, many will benefit and flourish. People such as these, who have internalized the ethic of universal love, promote the survival of humanity.

Gandhi, for example, dedicated himself to serving humanity and improving the well-being of our global community. But the unconditional love that guided him could be seen much earlier in his life, when Gandhi served as a soldier. When he risked his life to save his fellow soldiers on the battlefield as a medic on the British side of the Boer War, he displayed the fury that motivates us to help our loved ones. Louis Fischer, a reporter who knew Gandhi, described how he remained strong and courageous during the Boer War, despite the harsh circumstances surrounding him. By being loving, he was capable of being brave.

Gandhi led his men on to the battlefield. For days, under the fire of enemy guns, they carried moaning soldiers to the base hospital. "After a night's work which had shattered men with much bigger frames," Mr. Stent recalled, "I came across Gandhi in the early morning sitting by the roadside eating a regulation army biscuit. Every man in Buller's force was dull and depressed, and damnation was invoked on everything. But Gandhi was stoical in his bearing, cheerful, and confident in his conversations, and had a kindly eye. He did one good." He wore a khaki uniform, a jaunty, broad-brimmed cowboy felt hat, a Red Cross armband, and a drooping mustache. When the corps was disbanded it was mentioned in dispatches and Gandhi and several comrades were awarded the War Medal.[12]

Unconditional love was the source of Gandhi's courage. When people embrace the power of unconditional love, they gain the strength to serve their community and overcome adversity just like Gandhi, and they become much stronger than those who are filled with hatred. Hatred weakens a person by inflicting him with its painful burn. Hatred also makes a person as dangerous to himself as to others. The severity of Hitler's destructive attitude caused him to be insecure, terrified, and paranoid. Toward the end of World War II, Hitler slipped into insanity and killed himself. Mahatma Gandhi and Martin Luther King Jr., on the other hand, remained courageous despite countless threats upon their lives.

Albert Einstein understood that hatred is a counterproductive attitude that endangers the survival of humanity. Too many people do not understand the importance of compassion and cooperation, he explained, because they believe the illusions of social Darwinism, an idea that Darwin himself never advocated. Einstein said:

> Darwin's theory of the struggle for existence and the selectivity connected with it has by many people been cited as authorization of the encouragement of the spirit of competition. Some people also in such a way have tried to prove pseudo-scientifically the necessity of the destructive economic struggle of competition between individuals. But this is wrong, because man owes his strength in the struggle for existence to the fact that he is a socially living animal. As little as a battle between single ants of an ant hill is essential for survival, just so little is this the case with the individual members of a human community.[13]

The fact that human beings have survived in communities for thousands of years proves that unconditional love is more powerful than hatred. If human beings did not have a stronger inclination to cooperate, care for each other, and survive rather than to wage war, we would not be alive to discuss these ideas today.

These ideas show that world peace is possible. This possibility is not based on my opinion, because it is a fact that war drives people insane, that the greatest problem of every army is how to stop soldiers from running away, that being loving allows us to be brave, that cooperation is the key to our survival, that unconditional love builds an indestructible bond between people, that we have a stronger instinct to posture than to kill, that fury motivates us to protect our loved ones, that hatred is always painful, that unconditional love is inherently joyful, and that unconditional love is stronger than hatred. This is simply who we are and these facts prove that human beings are not naturally violent. War is not inevitable, and we all have the power to help end war and ensure the survival of humanity.

THE SURVIVAL OF HUMANITY

In the twenty-first century, humanity has become so interconnected that we are now a global community in which the fate of every human being is tied to the fate of our planet. In this interconnected world, war threatens our very survival, because war is more dangerous than ever.

A hundred years ago human beings were developing automatic machine guns. Today we have enough nuclear weapons to destroy the world several times over. For much of the twentieth century two nuclear superpowers held our planet hostage. Today many countries wish to acquire nuclear weapons. As technology continues to evolve, who can predict how destructive weapons will be a hundred years from now? Because war has become so devastating, ending war is no longer just a moral issue, but an issue that will determine the survival of humanity. Accordingly, the question *will war ever end?* can be reworded: *will humanity survive or will we destroy ourselves?*

Slavery existed on a global scale for thousands of years, but due to the courageous actions of our ancestors who fought this injustice, no country today sanctions slavery. Together we have the capacity to create a world where countries no longer sanction war. This is possible because human beings are not naturally violent, war strays so far from our peaceful survival instincts that it drives people insane, and unlike slavery, war is not just a moral issue, but a matter of our survival. By learning from the soldiers of peace who came before us, we will better understand how together we can fight for our survival.

SOLDIERS OF PEACE

I was a senior at West Point on the morning of September 11, 2001. Like any other day, I had woken up that morning with too little sleep, eaten breakfast too fast, and hurried to my class on national security, where I sat taking notes with a dozen other West Point cadets. While our professor was speaking, another teacher walked into the classroom and told him to turn on the television. In silence, all of us watched as the second plane hit the World Trade Center. As students of American foreign policy, we all knew what this meant. We would be going to war.

During the next several years, I saw my friends and comrades deploy to Afghanistan and Iraq, as the United States struggled to fight an expanding war on terrorism. To protect its citizens from the threats it perceived, the U.S. government relied upon a foreign policy of military might. At West Point, I was taught that military might has severe limitations, because armies are trained to conquer and destroy, not to build nations. I also learned that a war on terrorism can never be won with an army alone, because terrorism is not a place we can occupy or a dictator we can overthrow. Terrorism is a tactic. Terrorism is an idea, and no amount of military might can destroy an idea.

The idea of terrorism arises from despair, feeds on fear, and lacks unconditional love for human life. Because it uses hatred to perpetuate violence, terrorism is an idea that not only threatens our country, but the survival of humanity. To fight this idea, the U.S. government has deployed the most technologically advanced army in history, but it does not have enough soldiers to wage war on multiple fronts. I have seen firsthand how our military has been strained, how multiple deployments have pushed many soldiers to the breaking point, and how our military's medical care system was not prepared to handle the influx of physically and emotionally wounded soldiers returning from overseas.

If we are going to win the war on terrorism and overcome the challenges that threaten us in the twenty-first century, the United States will require many more soldiers, and not just soldiers who are armed with guns.

The first soldier of peace was Socrates, who abandoned his spear and armed himself with the power of words and ideas. Before he changed history as a soldier of peace, Socrates served as a soldier on the battlefield when he fought for Athens. Alcibiades, whose life Socrates once saved, described his heroism:

> During the battle after which the generals awarded me the prize for bravery, it was Socrates, no one else, who rescued me. He wasn't prepared to leave me when I was wounded and so he saved my life as well as my armor and weapons. I actually told the generals to award the prize for bravery on that occasion to you, Socrates . . . But when the generals wanted to award the prize to me, influenced by my social status, you yourself were keener than the generals that I should receive it.[14]

On the battlefield, Socrates displayed fury by saving Alcibiades' life, but in civil society, Socrates showed that when soldiers of peace love their country, they gain the strength to serve their community and improve their society. When I was deployed in Iraq and had a chance to watch American news channels, I heard commentators say that if we question or criticize our government, we do not love America and are being unpatriotic. They believed that patriotism meant waving a flag and being blindly obedient, but as Socrates and others have shown, this is not what it means to love our country.

What does it mean to truly love our country? We can better understand love of country by realizing what it means to love a child. Parents who love their children will try to correct a child caught stealing, abusing people, or being dishonest. For parents who do not truly love their children, apathy will cause them not to care, enabling their children to get away with anything. In this same way, if we love our country we will do our best to improve it. We will try to make America a better place for everyone, as courageous citizens have always done.

Since our country's founding, brave patriots have worked to give us the many freedoms we enjoy today. Two hundred years ago in America, anyone who was not a white, male landowner suffered oppression. During this era, the majority of people lacked the right to vote, and many Americans lived as slaves. Our country is much more humane today than it was then. This happened because courageous citizens such as Martin Luther King Jr., Mark Twain, Helen Keller, Susan B. Anthony, Woody Guthrie, Smedley Butler[15], Henry David Thoreau, and many others struggled to make our country a better place for all people.

Because of the countless responsible Americans who loved and were therefore willing to question, constructively criticize, and improve their country, America has made a lot of progress. When my father was drafted into the army in 1949, the military was segregated because the government upheld an official policy that viewed African Americans as inferior and subhuman. At the turn of the previous century, the government would not allow women to vote, and only fifty years prior to that, the government supported and protected slavery.

These examples of progress show that in addition to creating an indestructible bond, unconditional love also encourages us to work and sacrifice for the well-being of others. Because Socrates loved his country he was willing to work and sacrifice to improve it, even at great personal risk.

Until his death in 399 BC, Socrates served his country with the power of words and ideas. As a soldier of peace, he tried to improve his society by expressing the importance of courage, awareness, and selfless service not only in words, but through actions. Although the citizens of Athens suffered from greed and ignorance, Socrates said:

> My very good friend, you are an Athenian and belong to a city which is the greatest and most famous in the world for its wisdom and strength. Are you not ashamed that you give your attention to acquiring as much money as possible, and similarly with reputation and honor, and give no attention or thought to truth and understanding and the perfection of your soul? . . . Wealth does

not bring goodness, but goodness brings wealth and every other blessing, both to the individual and to the state.[16]

Every day, Socrates shared ideas with people as he walked through the streets of Athens. Because he pondered and questioned everything, this soldier of peace became an annoyance to those in power. As a consequence, at the age of seventy he was put on trial for challenging the greed and ignorance of his society, and the penalty demanded was death. After listening to hours of testimony in the civic center of Athens, a jury of five hundred people voted in favor of executing Socrates. Not surprised by this decision, Socrates bravely discussed his impending execution and a soldier's duty to fight for justice and truth.

In battle it is often obvious that you could escape being killed by giving up your arms and throwing yourself upon the mercy of your pursuers; and in every kind of danger there are plenty of devices for avoiding death if you are unscrupulous enough to stop at nothing. But I suggest, gentlemen, that the difficulty is not so much to escape death; the real difficulty is to escape from wickedness, which is far more fleet of foot. In this present instance I, the slow old man, have been overtaken by the slower of the two, but my accusers, who are clever and quick, have been overtaken by the faster: by iniquity. When I leave this court I shall go away condemned by you to death, but they will go away convicted by Truth herself of depravity and injustice . . . If you expect to stop denunciation of your wrong way of life by putting people to death, there is something amiss with your reasoning.[17]

Socrates died because he tried to improve his society and defend freedom of speech, but he lives on through us because his sacrifice inspired the many liberties we enjoy today. Considered the founder of Western philosophy, this soldier of peace began a new tradition of rational thought, critical thinking, and scientific inquiry that significantly changed the course of human history. The freedoms within our democracy, for example, were first instituted by our founding fathers, who were students of Western philosophy. Thomas Jefferson said, "The superlative wisdom of Socrates is testified by all antiquity . . ."[18]

Socrates shaped the course of history not by fighting for a bloody revolution, but by striving for a peaceful revolution in the minds and hearts of his people. His only weapon on the streets of ancient Athens was the wisdom that he tirelessly shared with anyone willing to listen. Through his sacrifice, Socrates became Europe's first martyr, representing a new kind of hero in Western thinking. Before Socrates, many

Greek heroes consisted of mythical conquerors such as Achilles, who were admired for their courage during combat. Socrates represented a new kind of soldier—a soldier of peace—who fought for his ideals, had the courage of his convictions, and changed how people think for the better. In the Western world, Socrates became the first in a long line of peaceful heroes that would later include Martin Luther King Jr., Albert Schweitzer, Susan B. Anthony, and countless others.

After executing Socrates, the Athenians realized they had made a terrible mistake. Although they later built a statue to honor him, the true testament to Socrates' legacy can be found within the ideals of freedom, democracy, and justice that have shaped our country and world for the better. Because of him, we Americans have the freedom to peacefully improve our country without being executed by our government. This vast freedom not only shows how far we have risen toward the ideal of liberty, it gives us the power to keep rising higher.

In the twentieth century, soldiers of peace took this legacy to new heights. Socrates revealed how we can improve our society as individuals, but another group of soldiers demonstrated how we can work toward a brighter future as people united. The American soldiers who left their jobs behind to fight in World War I were paid little more than a dollar a day for their service to their country. Following World War I, the government promised that these veterans would receive adjusted compensation to pay for their lost wages while fighting overseas. However, this promise became known as the "Tombstone Bonus," because these veterans—many of them starving, in poverty, and even homeless because of the Great Depression—could not collect the wages owed to them until 1945, or when they died.

In the summer of 1932, at the height of the Great Depression, tens of thousands of World War I veterans peacefully marched on Washington, DC, with their families. Camping in a muddy area across the Anacostia River, the veterans built a community where white and black people lived, protested, and fought for justice together. Putting democracy into action by peacefully demonstrating outside the Capitol Building, they demanded urgent payment of the wages they had been promised. In their favor, the "Bonus Bill" had just been passed in the House of Representatives, which agreed to pay the owed wages immediately.

On June 17, 1932, thousands of veterans assembled on Capitol Hill where they tried to convince the Senate to support the bill passed by the House of Representatives. During the Senate debate, the senators could hear the shouts of the veterans: "The Yanks are starving! The Yanks are starving!" Despite these cries for justice, the Bonus Bill was overwhelmingly defeated in the Senate.

Following the Senate's decision, some of the officials in Washington expected the veterans gathered outside of the Capitol Building to riot. But the "Bonus Marchers" or "Bonus Army" as they had come to be known, did not resort to violence. Instead, they all sang "America the Beautiful" and dispersed from the Capitol Building peacefully.

Many of the marchers remained in Washington to continue their protest, but President Hoover soon ordered their evacuation. The U.S. Army used infantrymen carrying rifles and unsheathed bayonets, along with cavalry, tanks, and gas on the Bonus Marchers. These veterans, who had been gassed in Europe fighting on behalf of America, were now being gassed in our country's capital. During this assault, two Bonus Marchers were killed, hundreds more were injured, and their camps were burned and destroyed.

Following this atrocity, public sentiment turned in favor of the Bonus Marchers. Believing that the voice of suffering people should be heard in a true democracy, the Bonus Marchers returned to Washington every year. After four years of peaceful and democratic struggle, Congress passed the Bonus Bill, which paid much-needed wages to over four million veterans. This victory led to the GI Bill of Rights, passed in 1944, which helped World War II veterans go to college, obtain home loans, and readjust to civilian life after the war. By helping poor people go to college, the GI Bill of Rights also played a significant role in building America's middle class.[19]

The veterans assaulted in Washington were soldiers of peace who replaced their guns with civil action. They believed in the spirit of democracy, an ideal in which the strength of peaceful struggle can create positive change. Through their courage, the Bonus Marchers won a victory for justice that increased our freedom to publically demonstrate, thereby making it possible for members of the civil rights movement to peacefully march on Washington decades later.

While the Bonus Marchers helped build the foundation that made the civil rights movement successful, soldiers of peace such as Socrates inspired Gandhi, Martin Luther King Jr., and many others to also struggle for peace. Martin Luther King Jr. said:

> I have earnestly opposed violent tension, but there is a type of constructive, nonviolent tension which is necessary for growth . . . Socrates felt that it was necessary to create a tension in the mind so that individuals could rise from the bondage of myths and half-truths to the unfettered realm of creative analysis and objective appraisal . . . the kind of tension in society that will help men rise from the dark depths of prejudice and racism to the majestic heights of understanding and brotherhood.[20]

After serving in the Boer and Zulu wars as a soldier for the British Empire, Gandhi served humanity as a soldier of peace. To me, Gandhi's life is one of the most incredible David and Goliath stories in history. This humble man with few possessions defeated the most powerful empire on earth, helped free his people from colonial oppression, and produced peaceful tactics that forever changed our world.

When I studied military history at West Point, I realized how brilliant these peaceful tactics were. In Gandhi's creative forms of protest, such as his Salt March to the Sea, I saw a tactical and strategic genius. To me, Gandhi was to nonviolence as Hannibal, the skillful Carthaginian general who fought the Roman Empire, was to violence. Instead of swords and spears, Gandhi's weapons were love and understanding. Rather than a military campaign designed to kill his enemy, Gandhi waged a peaceful campaign that sought to transform his enemy into a friend. Because he loved his country along with our global human family, Gandhi possessed a magnitude of courage that rivaled that of even the most heroic general.

Throughout history, soldiers of peace have used their large brains and the strength of unconditional love and cooperation to shape our world for the better. Soldiers of peace have made a tremendous impact upon human civilization because they seek to create and build, not to destroy, and they understand that every person is a member of our global human family. In the fifth century BC, Socrates said, "I am not an Athenian or a Greek, but a citizen of the world." [21]

In the twenty-first century, humanity has become so interconnected that we are all citizens of the world, whether we recognize it or not. During the challenging years ahead, our planet will need soldiers of peace who understand this truth of our brotherhood, because our survival in an interconnected world will not depend upon our ability to wage war. The fate of humanity will depend upon our willingness to wage peace.

WAGING PEACE

To build a better world, soldiers of peace must use the creative power of peaceful means, rather than the destructive methods of violence. Martin Luther King Jr. explained:

> And the leaders of the world today talk eloquently about peace. Every time we drop our bombs in North Vietnam, President Johnson talks eloquently about peace. What is the problem? They are talking about peace as a distant goal, as an end we seek, but one day we must come to see that

peace is not merely a distant goal we seek, but that it is a means by which we arrive at that goal. We must pursue peaceful ends through peaceful means. All of this is saying that, in the final analysis, means and ends must cohere because the end is preexistent in the means, and ultimately destructive means cannot bring about constructive ends.[22]

History has shown that when people want to improve the world, peaceful means are more effective than guns and bombs, because violence has no creative power. Violence is only capable of tearing something down, while peaceful means have the power to create, nurture, and build. Because courageous people have used peaceful means, including democratic and civil actions, nonviolent protests, and the power of words and ideas to change how people think for the better, human civilization has come a long way since the life and death of Socrates.

In ancient Athens there were many more slaves than citizens, while women were severely oppressed and not even treated as human beings. Since then our ancestors abolished state-sanctioned slavery on a global scale during the past several hundred years, even though slavery built the economic backbone of many countries. Furthermore, women's rights have improved dramatically in many areas of the world because a few people were willing to wage peace rather than war.

Thomas Clarkson was one such person who improved our world by waging peace rather than war. Born in England in 1760, Clarkson was a devout Christian who dedicated his life to achieving liberty for all people. He played a prominent role in the abolition movements in Europe and the United States, but his journey began when he explored the issue of slavery as a student at Cambridge. In 1785 he entered a Latin essay contest, winning with the essay "Is It Lawful to Enslave the Unconsenting?"

This antislavery essay would change Clarkson's life. After he read his essay to an audience at the university's Senate House, Clarkson mounted his horse and proceeded to London to further his career in the church. Clarkson was already a deacon in the Church of England, but on his way to London the well-being of humanity became more important than his career. Like Saul's conversion on the road to Damascus, Clarkson had an epiphany that would transform not only him, but the entire world.[23]

"Coming in sight of Wades Mill in Hertfordshire," Clarkson wrote, "I sat down disconsolate on the turf by the roadside and held my horse. Here a thought came into my mind, that if the contents of the Essay were true, it was time some person should see these calamities to their end."[24] During this brief moment, one person decided to make the ideal of liberty a reality for all people and end one of history's greatest injustices. In his book *Bury the Chains*, Adam Hochschild said, "If there is a single moment at which the antislavery movement became inevitable, it was the day in June 1785 when Thomas Clarkson sat down by the side of the road at Wades Mill."[25]

When Clarkson decided to wage peace by fighting to free all slaves, many people thought he would never succeed, because state-sanctioned slavery had existed on a global scale for thousands of years. However, Clarkson showed that one person can begin a peaceful revolution and unravel an injustice that has existed since the beginning of recorded history. Because of Clarkson and other peaceful heroes who struggled valiantly with him, no government in the world today openly supports the injustice of slavery. Clarkson showed that in any era, peaceful means have the power to change our world for the better.

The American Civil War, for example, did not give African Americans their full freedom. Similar to the peaceful protests and boycotts of the British abolitionists, it took a peaceful movement in the 1950s and 1960s to give African Americans their fundamental human rights. If we are willing to use our large brains and the strength of unconditional love to change the world, we can continue the legacy of peace that echoes through the actions of Socrates, Clarkson, and many others. Like them, we can wage peace by not only standing up for justice, but by joining with people who understand that peaceful means can create, nurture, and build a better world.

After risking his life by opposing the highly profitable slave trade, Clarkson joined with Christians such as the Quakers. In the eighteenth century, the Quakers were also on a mission to end slavery and achieve liberty for all people. Clarkson wrote, "Such have been the exertions of the Quakers in the cause of humanity and virtue. They are still prosecuting, as far as they are able, their benevolent design . . . They are acting consistently with the principles of religion. They will find a reward in their own consciences . . ."[26]

Waging peace means that we take action and that "we prosecute, as far as we are able, our benevolent design" for a peaceful world. If we prosecute our benevolent design for a peaceful world through peaceful means, then another injustice that has plagued humanity for thousands of years, existing on as massive a scale as slavery, may also meet its demise. Together, we can take human civilization to new heights by ending the injustice of war that has been with us for far too long.

To achieve these heights, we must realize that, for many reasons, waging peace is more effective than waging war. By exploring human nature we have learned that unconditional love is stronger than hatred, and by looking at history, we have seen that peaceful means are more powerful than violent methods. Because people waged peace, they created the ideals, hopes, and dreams that can never be torn down by violence. Although Socrates was executed, Martin Luther King Jr. and Gandhi were assassinated, and the Bonus Marchers were attacked, violence could not silence the ideals they stood for. Unlike violence, which is only capable of destruction, ideals such as freedom, justice, and peace have built our human civilization. These ideals have the strength to not only create and endure, but to grow stronger with each successive generation.

For example, in only a few hundred years the right to vote, freedom of religion, freedom of speech, freedom of assembly, freedom of the press, democracy, and women's and civil rights have become widespread. In only two hundred years, America has journeyed from a country where all people except white, male landowners were oppressed, to a society where I could graduate from West Point and write these words today, despite having grown up in Alabama part African American, part Asian.

If we are going to continue this journey toward global peace and prosperity, we must unite and wage peace whether we are soldiers such as Socrates or civilians such as Thomas Clarkson. In the twenty-first century, terrorism is one of many challenges we must overcome to not only achieve global peace and prosperity, but to survive. Despite these dangers, history has shown that because unconditional love and cooperation are so powerful, when just a few people are willing to wage peace, what once seemed impossible can happen on an immense scale.

Gopal Krishna Gokhale, the leader of the Indian nationalist movement in India, visited Gandhi in 1912 and asked him for a list of his reliable resisters who were willing to challenge the British Empire. Gokhale expected a long list of resisters who would challenge the most powerful empire on earth, but Gandhi only provided sixty-six names, admitting that this number might drop to sixteen. Gandhi called this his "army of peace." Understanding that a few people willing to wage peace are capable of changing the world, Gandhi never flinched, even when his supporters were few in number. Gandhi was certain that the strength of unconditional love would defeat injustice.[27]

The anthropologist Margaret Mead said, "Never doubt that a small group of thoughtful, committed citizens can change the world. Indeed, it's the only thing that ever has."[28] Similar to the movements that abolished slavery and gave African Americans their civil rights, the women's rights movement in America gained women the right to vote not because everyone participated in it, but because a small percentage of the population was willing to wage peace and make a difference. These victories reveal that if we are determined to take small yet significant steps toward a better world, we can bring humanity closer and closer toward the end of war and a global civilization of peace and prosperity.

My experiences as a child in Alabama, a student at West Point, and a soldier in Baghdad have caused my obsession with war to grow into my hope that, together, we can wage peace and end war in the twenty-first century. In these pages we have taken a first step on this journey by expressing a new vision of peace and human nature. This vision explains why human beings are not naturally violent, war is not inevitable, and how peace is not just a destination, but a road that we must walk if we are going to overcome the challenges that threaten us today.

THE FIRST STEP ON THE ROAD TO PEACE

Trying to end war without understanding human nature is like trying to go to the moon without understanding the laws of physics. Now that we have better defined human nature and our potential for peace, we have taken a first and crucial step on our journey toward creating a more peaceful world. To build this brighter future, we must rely on unconditional love and our large brains, rather than hatred and violence. We must remember that war never fully solves a problem and that peaceful ends always require peaceful means.

My experiences in the military have taught me not only that war can end through peaceful means, but that war *must* end if humanity is going to survive in the twenty-first century and beyond. The suffering of my parents and the trauma I endured during my youth are responsible for these realizations and my obsession with understanding war. Because these experiences led to a deeper understanding of what it means to be a human being, I now have an obsession with transforming our shared hope for a peaceful world into a brighter future.

Although I have learned that war is not inevitable, I have realized that a peaceful future is also not inevitable. War will not magically end on its own, and our world will never know peace if we sit around and do nothing. War will only end if we end it. War will only end if we stand up and make a difference, if we take crucial steps to ensure our survival and prosperity as a global community.

Exploring human nature to explain why we are not naturally violent opens up a wide range of hopeful possibilities for our future, but this is just one among many necessary steps on our journey toward global peace and prosperity. For us to truly answer the question, *will war ever end?* we must create world peace by continuing this journey and cooperating with the countless people who still have faith in humanity. By working together, we can transform our shared hope for a peaceful world into a reality within our reach.

TOWARD A NEW ENLIGHTENMENT

As a small boy, I was obsessed with learning if war will ever end, but as I grew into a young adult, I became obsessed with discovering how we can heal the causes of violence and conflict. When I was a child, I heard solutions to these problems that disappointed me. I often heard people say, for example, that we could end war by creating a world where people are no longer willing to wage war. Even today, I hear people say that we can end war by creating a world where everyone is willing to live in harmony and settle their differences without resorting to violence. These answers disappointed me because such a world is a goal, an objective, an end-state, and these answers do not address the crucial question, what means can we use to approach this end-state?

When someone says that we can end war by creating a world where people are no longer willing to wage war, it is like saying, "We can cure polio by finding a cure for polio." Saying that we can end war by creating a world where everyone is willing to live in harmony does not actually explain how we will make this happen. To find a vaccine for polio, for example, people had to begin by studying and understanding the disease. Only then could they discover the means to prevent it. By beginning to study and understand the true nature of war in these pages, we are taking a first step on the journey to heal the causes of violence and end war on a global scale.

To end war on a global scale, we must move beyond well-intentioned but inadequate answers that transform the ideal of peace into a cliché so often and widely mocked as a naïve dream. Peace ceases to be a cliché only when we have a thorough understanding of war, violence, and their underlying causes, just as doctors are only capable of understanding health once they understand illness, disease, and their underlying causes. If certain basic facts about war are not understood, we cannot fully understand what makes peace so practical, possible, and necessary.

Proving that human beings are naturally peaceful is just one basic fact and an important step in the right direction. Today, many people believe the myth that human beings are naturally violent. This myth continues to have devastating consequences. When I studied psychology at West Point, I learned about a phenomenon called *self-fulfilling prophecy* that can be illustrated with the following example. If you constantly tell a young child he is stupid, he will begin to believe he is stupid, even if he is very intelligent. As a consequence, this false belief will have a negative impact on his behavior and performance. Similarly, if people are told they are naturally violent, that violence is a necessary expression of our humanity, and that "only the dead have seen the end of war," then they will behave more violently. Peace will not only seem unrealistic and unattainable to them, but absurd.

When people believe that human beings are naturally violent, war is rarely viewed as a disaster that we are powerful enough to prevent; instead, it is seen as an integral part of life that we are helpless to stop. In these pages, however, we have shown that hatred and violence, like an illness, are not necessary expressions of our humanity but occur when something has gone terribly wrong. By improving our understanding of human nature we can begin not only to understand what has gone wrong when war occurs, but how we can prevent the causes of violence and conflict.

In addition to war, slavery has also been supported and prolonged through an inaccurate understanding of human nature. Today if I said, "People do not want to be slaves; human beings have an innate yearning for freedom, and to enslave a group of people, harsh techniques must be used to break their will and suppress their human nature," then most of us would say this is obvious and common sense. But this was not common sense several hundred years ago.

For centuries, many people believed that it was in the nature of some races and ethnicities to live as slaves. Many of these people even believed that most slaves were happy being slaves. This view was challenged when the Renaissance and Enlightenment movements changed how people thought and saw the world, giving birth to the idea of freedom. In the East, freedom had been understood as liberation from inner suffering, but this new Western concept of freedom meant that every person had an inalienable right to live free from outer oppression. The American Declaration of Independence, itself a product of the Enlightenment, echoed this bold new idea that every person has a right to "life, liberty, and the pursuit of happiness."

Throughout history, people have fought for their personal, tribal, and national freedom, but the idea of universal human freedom did not become a widespread movement until the Enlightenment of the eighteenth century. Although the Athenians and Spartans defended their freedom against the Persians, they did not believe every human being had a right to live free from oppression. Instead, they believed that Greeks should not be slaves, because the Greeks should be the slave masters.

The ancient Greeks did not abolish slavery, but

when the Declaration of Independence stated that "all men are created equal" and that people have a right to "life, liberty, and the pursuit of happiness," it sowed the seeds for the eventual abolition of slavery in America. As the country progressed, it became increasingly difficult to continue slavery with these Enlightenment ideals embodied in the Declaration of Independence.

The philosophers who created these Enlightenment ideals persuaded Europeans that it is human nature to strive for freedom. Gradually, this led many people to view slavery as unnatural. Furthermore, after Europeans had witnessed the American Revolution, French Revolution, and numerous slave revolts around the world, the abolition of slavery began to seem not only logical to them, but inevitable.

Today, many people believe the myth that human beings are naturally violent and that war is an inescapable part of human nature, just as in the past many people believed the myth that it was in the nature of some races and ethnicities to live as slaves. I hope that through our efforts, saying that human beings are naturally violent will sound as absurd as saying that most slaves are happy being slaves or the sun revolves around the earth.

Of course, many people today want to believe that human beings are naturally peaceful, but they are unable to reconcile why war exists if this belief is true. Our understanding that human beings are naturally peaceful, on the other hand, is not based solely on a belief. We have overwhelming evidence that it is true. Consequently, when I say that human beings are naturally peaceful, it is not a matter of blind faith. I say this with the same confidence I would have when proclaiming that two plus two equals four.

As I have already mentioned, explaining why human beings are naturally peaceful is only the first step. Together, we must continue on the road to peace by exploring how we can heal the causes of violence and conflict. Later on, we will journey beyond the concepts presented in *Will War Ever End?* by explaining why violence occurs and how we can end the wars between countries, our ongoing war with nature, and the suffering in our hearts. We will also learn why human beings are not naturally greedy or selfish, and why generosity and kindness are necessary for human survival.

THE NEXT STEP

Before exploring these new concepts, what can we all do now to make a difference? To make a difference in the lives of those around us, we can discuss this first step with our friends and family, we can form small groups to talk about the nature of war and the possibility of peace, and we can share these hopeful ideas with everyone we know. Discussing and sharing ideas, after all, is the key to progress. Throughout history, all progress has resulted from new ideas that change how people think for the better.

The abolition of slavery, right to vote, freedom of religion, freedom of speech, freedom of assembly, freedom of the press, democracy, and women's and civil rights became widespread, for example, because new ideas changed how people thought and perceived their humanity. These liberties do not yet exist everywhere, because progress is a gradual process and the personal responsibility of every citizen of the world.

Although oppression and illegal forms of slavery still exist, for instance, the fact that slavery has been greatly reduced and deemed illegal shows that our civilization has made tremendous progress in the right direction. As citizens of the world, we not only have a responsibility to continue moving in this direction, but to blaze new trails with ideas that can give us a better understanding of human nature, war, and peace.

To help us blaze these trails, we are living in an era that gives us a greater chance of ending war than any in the past. We are living during the information revolution, a time when the Internet and other means of electronic communication can have as big an impact on humanity as the agricultural and industrial revolutions.

During the Enlightenment of the eighteenth century, the ideas that led to the abolition of slavery and the rise of our modern liberties were spread by people riding on horseback from town to town. Many of the people in these towns were not even able to read; they heard new ideas only through word of mouth. Today during the information revolution, ideas can circle the globe at the speed of light, more people than ever are literate, and our world is truly connected and ready for a new Enlightenment. Not only are we ready in fact, but people all over the world are hungry for a global peace movement that will end war once and for all.

To end war once and for all, we have taken the first step toward a new Enlightenment that will change how people understand human nature, war, and peace, just as the first Enlightenment changed how people understood slavery and freedom. Together, by sharing and discussing these ideas, we can take the next step. We can bring humanity toward a new vision of peace for the twenty-first century. We can journey toward a global civilization of peace and prosperity, and begin a revolution of ideas that will show us all how the living can also see the end of war.

War Veterans Speak

General Dwight D. Eisenhower: Veteran of World War II

"Disarmament, with mutual honor and confidence, is a continuing imperative. Together we must learn how to compose differences, not with arms, but with intellect and decent purpose. As one who has witnessed the horror and the lingering sadness of war—as one who knows that another war could utterly destroy this civilization which has been so slowly and painfully built over thousands of years—I wish I could say tonight that a lasting peace is in sight. Happily, I can say that war has been avoided. Steady progress toward our ultimate goal has been made. But, so much remains to be done. As a private citizen, I shall never cease to do what little I can to help the world advance along that road . . . We pray . . . that, in the goodness of time, all peoples will come to live together in a peace guaranteed by the binding force of mutual respect and love."[29]

"Every gun that is made, every warship launched, every rocket fired signifies, in the final sense, a theft from those who hunger and are not fed, those who are cold and are not clothed. This world in arms is not spending money alone. It is spending the sweat of its laborers, the genius of its scientists, the hopes of its children. The cost of one modern heavy bomber is this: a modern brick school in more than 30 cities. It is two electric power plants, each serving a town of 60,000 population. It is two fine, fully equipped hospitals. It is some 50 miles of concrete highway. We pay for a single fighter with a half million bushels of wheat. We pay for a single destroyer with new homes that could have housed more than 8,000 people. This, I repeat, is the best way of life to be found on the road the world has been taking. This is not a way of life at all, in any true sense. Under the cloud of threatening war, it is humanity hanging from a cross of iron."[30]

George Orwell: Veteran of the Spanish Civil War

"One of the most horrible features of war is that all the war-propaganda, all the screaming and lies and hatred, comes invariably from people who are not fighting."[31]

"The essential act of war is destruction, not necessarily of human lives, but of the products of human labour. War is a way of shattering to pieces, or pouring into the stratosphere, or sinking in the depths of the sea, materials which might otherwise be used to make the masses too comfortable, and hence, in the long run, too intelligent."[32]

General Omar Bradley: Veteran of World War II

"It is easy for us who are living to honor the sacrifices of those who are dead. For it helps us to assuage the guilt we should feel in their presence. Wars can be prevented just as surely as they are provoked, and therefore we who fail to prevent them share in guilt for the dead."[33]

"Now new weapons have made the risk of war a suicidal hazard. . . . Modern war visits destruction on the victor and the vanquished alike. Our only complete assurance of surviving World War III is to halt it before it starts." [34]

Major General Smedley Butler: Veteran of the Boxer Rebellion, World War I, and other conflicts

"War is a racket. It always has been . . . A racket is best described, I believe, as something that is not what it seems to the majority of the people. Only a small 'inside' group knows what it is about. It is conducted for the benefit of the very few, at the expense of the very many. Out of war a few people make huge fortunes. In the World War [I] a mere handful garnered the profits of the conflict. At least 21,000 new millionaires and billionaires were made in the United States during the World War . . . How many of these new millionaires shouldered a rifle? How many of them dug a trench? How many of them knew what it meant to go hungry in a rat-infested dug-out? How many of them spent sleepless, frightened nights, ducking shells and shrapnel and machine gun bullets? How many of them parried a bayonet thrust of an enemy? How many of them were wounded or killed in battle?"[35]

"The general public shoulders the bill [of war]. And what is this bill? This bill renders a horrible accounting. Newly placed gravestones. Mangled bodies. Shattered minds. Broken hearts and homes. Economic instability. Depression and all its attendant miseries. Back-breaking taxation for generations and generations . . . It would have been far cheaper (not to say safer) for the average American who pays the bills to stay out of foreign entanglements. For a very few this racket, like bootlegging and other underworld rackets, brings fancy profits, but the cost of operations is always transferred to the people—who do not profit . . . But the soldier pays the biggest part of the bill. If you don't believe this, visit the American cemeteries on the battlefields abroad. Or visit any of the veteran's hospitals in the United States."[36]

Leo Tolstoy: Veteran of the Crimean War

"But in all history there is no war which was not hatched by the governments, the governments alone, independent of the interests of the people, to whom war is always pernicious even when successful."[37]

"War, the thing for the sake of which all the nations of the earth—millions and millions of people—place at the uncontrolled disposal of a few men or sometimes only one man, not merely milliards of rubles, talers, francs or yen (representing a very large share of their labor), but also their very lives."[38]

Antoine de Saint-Exupéry: Veteran of World War II (killed in action)

"The adventure of war? Where is there adventure in war? . . . I have had adventures—pioneering mail lines; being forced down among rebellious Arabs in the Sahara; flying the Andes. But war is not a true adventure. It is a mere ersatz [counterfeit]. Where ties are established, where problems are set, where creation is stimulated—there you have adventure. But there is no adventure in heads-or-tails, in betting that the toss will come out life or death. War is not an adventure. It is a disease."[39]

"During the day my body was available for transformation into a lair of agony and undeserved laceration. During the day my body was not mine. Was no longer mine. Any of its members might at any moment be commandeered; its blood might at any moment be drawn off without my acquiescence. For it is another consequence of war that the soldier's body becomes a stock of accessories that are no longer his property. The bailiff arrives and demands a pair of eyes—you yield up the gift of sight. The bailiff arrives and demands a pair of legs—you yield up the gift of movement."[40]

Mahatma Gandhi: Veteran of the Boer and Zulu Wars

"I am not a visionary. I claim to be a practical idealist. The religion of nonviolence is not meant merely for the rishis [sages] and saints. It is meant for the common people as well. Nonviolence is the law of our species as violence is the law of the brute. The spirit lies dormant in the brute and he knows no law but that of physical might. The dignity of man requires obedience to a higher law—to the strength of the spirit."[41]

"I do believe that all God's creatures have the right to live as much as we have. Instead of prescribing the killing of the so-called injurious fellow creatures of ours as a duty, if men of knowledge had devoted their gifts to discovering ways of dealing with them otherwise than by killing them, we would be living in a world befitting our status as men—animals endowed with reason and the power of choosing between good and evil, right and wrong, violence and nonviolence, truth and untruth."[42]

NOTES

1. Robert Pearce, ed., *The Sayings of Leo Tolstoy* (London: Duckworth, 1995), p. 41.

2. Address by General of the Army Douglas MacArthur to the Corps of Cadets on accepting the Thayer Award. MacArthur Foundation, www.westpoint.org/real/macarthur_address.html.

3. Ibid. MacArthur incorrectly attributed this quotation to Plato.

4. Lt. Col. Dave Grossman, *On Killing: The Psychological Cost of Learning to Kill in War and Society* (Boston: Little, Brown and Company, 1995), p. 50.

5. Floyd H. Ross and Tynette Hills, *The Great Religions by Which Men Live* (New York: Beacon Press, 1956), p. 80.

6. Aeschylus, *The Persians*, trans. Robert Potter. http://etext.library.adelaide.edu.au/a/aeschylus/persians/. I have replaced the word thralldom with oppression.

7. Office of Medical History, listing on Frederick C. Murphy. http://history.amedd.army.mil/moh/murphyf.htm.

8. Lt. Col. Dave Grossman, *On Killing: The Psychological Cost of Learning to Kill in War and Society* (Boston: Little, Brown and Company, 1995), p. 8.

9. Ibid., p. 9.

10. *War Dogs, America's Forgotten Heroes: The Untold Story of Dogs in Combat*, narr. Martin Sheen, VHS (GRB, Nature's Recipe Pet Foods, 1999).

11. *Tibet: Cry of the Snow Lion*, DVD (Earthworks Films/Zambuling Pictures, Inc., 2002)

12. Louis Fischer, *Gandhi: His Life and Message for the World* (New York: New American Library, 1982), pp. 27–28.

13. Albert Einstein, *Ideas and Opinions*, ed. Cal Seelig (New York: Three Rivers Press, 1982), p. 62.

14. Plato, *The Symposium*, trans. Christopher Gill (New York: Penguin Books, 1999), p. 60.

15. Smedley Butler (1881–1940) was a major general in the U.S.

Marines and twice received the Medal of Honor. At the time of his death, he was the most decorated marine in U.S. history. An outspoken critic of U.S. foreign policy and author of *War Is a Racket*, Butler argued against the strong influence of corporate interests that leads to U.S. military intervention overseas.

16. Plato, *The Last Days of Socrates*, trans. Hugh Tredennick and Harold Tarrant (New York: Penguin Books, 1993), p. 53.

17. Ibid., pp. 64, 65.

18. Thomas Jefferson, letters "Jesus and the Jews" to William Short, from the Library of America edition of Jefferson's writings, ed. Merrill D. Peterson.http://www.positiveatheism.org/hist/jeff1435.htm.

19. PBS Home Video (DVD): *The March of the Bonus Army*, Paul Dickson and Thomas B. Allen, 2006; *The Bonus Army: An American Epic* (New York: Walker and Company, 2004)

20. King, Martin Luther Jr., *The Autobiography of Martin Luther King Jr.*, (New York: Warner Books, 1998), p. 191.

21. Plutarch, *Of Banishment*. Online Library of Liberty, http://oll.libertyfund.org/?option=com_staticxt&staticfile=show.php%3Ftitle=1213&chapter=91778&layout=html&Itemid=27.

22. Martin Luther King Jr., Christmas sermon, December 24,1967. http://mlk-pp01.stanford.edu /index.php/resources/article/king_quotes_on_war_and_peace/

23. Adam Hochschild, *Bury the Chains*, (New York: Houghton Mifflin Company, 2005), p. 89.

24. Ibid.

25. Ibid.

26. Thomas Clarkson, "An Essay on the Slavery and Commerce of the Human Species, Particularly the African." The Project Gutenberg EBook, http://www.gutenberg.org/files/10611/10611-h/10611-h.htm.

27. Louis Fischer, *Gandhi: His Life and Message for the World* (New York: New American Library, 1982), p. 43

28. Adam Hochschild, *Bury the Chains*, (New York: Houghton Mifflin Company, 2005), p. 7.

29. Dwight D. Eisenhower, his farewell address to the nation, 1961. http://mcadams.posc.mu.edu/ike.htm.

30. Dwight D. Eisenhower, "The Chance for Speech," speech de-

livered before the American Society of Newspaper Editors, 1953. http://www.informationclearinghouse.info/article9743.htm.

31. George Orwell, *Homage to Catalonia*. Google Books, p. 65, http://books.google.com/books?id=d2rXwFdzuo8C&pg=PA65&lpg =PA65&dq=All+the+warpropaganda,+all+the+screaming+and+lies+ and+hatred,+comes+invariably+from+people+who+are+not+ fighting.&source=web&ots=COPjYOuvo3&sig=52dOmDInN7lz6 zlCnnRN_2xtvW08&hl=en&sa=X&oi=book_result&resnum=2&ct =result#PPA65,M1.

32. George Orwell, *1984*, (New York: Signet Classic, 1977), p. 157.

33. General Omar Bradley, 1948 Memorial Day address at Long Meadow, MA, http://www.guidepostsmag.com/personal-change/ personal-change-archive/?i=2208&page=1.

34. Ibid.

35. Brigadier General Smedley D. Butler, *War Is a Racket: The Antiwar Classic by America's Most Decorated Soldier* (Los Angeles: Feral House, 2003), p. 23.

36. Ibid., pp. 24, 26, 33.

37. Leo Tolstoy, excerpt from "On Patriotism." http://www. panarchy.org/tolstoy/1894.eng.html.

38. Leo Tolstoy, his last message to mankind, written for the 18th International Peace Congress held at Stockholm in 1909. http://www.jesusradicals.com/library/tolstoy/last.html.

39. Antoine de Saint-Exupéry, *Flight to Arras*, trans. Lewis Galantiére (New York: Reynal and Hitchcock, 1942), pp. 75, 81.

40. Ibid., p. 83.

41. Richard Attenborough, *The Words of Gandhi* (New York: Newmarket Press, 2000), p. 41.

42. Ibid., p. 91.

BIBLIOGRAPHY

Aeschylus, *The Persians*. Translated by Robert Potter. http://etext.library.adelaide.edu.au/a/aeschylus/persians/.

Attenborough, Richard. *The Words of Gandhi*. New York: Newmarket Press, 2000.

Bradley, Omar. 1948 Memorial Day address at Long Meadow, Massachusetts. http://www.guidepostsmag.com/personal-change/personal-change-archive/?i=2208&page=1.

Butler, Smedley D. *War Is a Racket: The Antiwar Classic by America's Most Decorated Soldier*. Los Angeles: Feral House, 2003.

Clarkson, Thomas. "An Essay on the Slavery and Commerce of the Human Species, Particularly the African." The Project Gutenberg EBook. http://www.gutenberg.org/files/10611/10611-h/10611-h.htm

Dickson, Paul and Thomas B. Allen. *The Bonus Army: An American Epic*. New York: Walker and Company, 2004.

Einstein, Albert. *Ideas and Opinions*. Edited by Cal Seelig. New York: Three Rivers Press, 1982.

Eisenhower, Dwight D. "The Chance for Speech." Speech delivered before the American Society of Newspaper Editors, 1953. http://www.informationclearinghouse.info/article9743.htm.

———. Eisenhower's farewell address to the nation. http://mcadams.posc.mu.edu/ike.htm

Fischer, Louis. Gandhi: *His Life and Message for the World*. New York: New American Library, 1982.

Grossman, Lt. Col. U.S. Army (ret.) Dave. *On Killing: The Psychological Cost of Learning to Kill in War and Society* . Boston: Little, Brown and Company, 1995.

Hochschild, Adam. *Bury the Chains.* New York: Houghton Mifflin Company, 2005.

Jefferson, Thomas. Letters "Jesus and the Jews" to William Short. Edited by Merrill D. Peterson. Library of America edition of Jefferson's writings.http://www.positiveatheism.org/hist/jeff1435.htm.

King, Martin Luther, Jr., *The Autobiography of Martin Luther King Jr.* New York: Warner Books, 1998.

King, Martin Luther Jr. Christmas sermon, 24 December 1967. http://mlk-kpp01.stanford.edu/index.php/resources/article/king_quotes_on_war_and_peace/.

MacArthur, Douglas. MacArthur Foundation. Address by General of the Army Douglas MacArthur to the Corps of Cadets on accepting the Thayer Award. http://www.west-point.org/real/macarthur_address.html.

The March of the Bonus Army. PBS Home Video. DVD. 2006

Office of Medical History. Listing on Frederick C. Murphy. http://history.amedd.army.mil/moh/murphyf.htm.

Orwell, George. *Homage to Catalonia.* Google Books, p. 65, http://books.google.com/books?id=d2rXwFdzuo8C&pg=PA65&lpg=PA65&dq=All+the+war-propaganda,+all+the+screaming+and+lies+and+hatred,+comes+invariably+from+people+who+are+not+fighting.&source=web&ots=COPjYOuvo3&sig=52dOmDInN7lz6zlCnnRN_2xtvW0&hl=en&sa=X&oi=book_result&resnum=2&ct=result#PPA65,M1.

Orwell, George. *1984.* New York: Signet Classic, 1977.

Pearce, Robert, ed., *The Sayings of Leo Tolstoy.* London: Duckworth, 1995.

Plato. *The Last Days of Socrates.* Translated by Hugh Tredennick and Harold Tarrant. New York: Penguin Books, 1993.

Plato. *The Symposium.* Translated by Christopher Gill. New York: Penguin Books, 1999.

Plutarch. *Of Banishment.* Online Library of Liberty. http://oll.libertyfund.org/?option=com_staticxt&staticfile=show.php%3Ftitle=1213&chapter=91778&layout=html&Itemid=27.

Ross, Floyd H., and Tynette Hills. *The Great Religions by Which Men Live.* New York: Beacon Press, 1956.

Saint-Exupéry, Antoine de. *Flight to Arras.* Translated by Lewis Galantiére. New York: Reynal and Hitchcock, 1942.

Tibet: Cry of the Snow Lion. DVD. Earthworks Films/Zambuling Pictures, Inc., 2002.

Tolstoy, Leo. Excerpt from "On Patriotism." http://www.panarchy.org/tolstoy/1894.eng.html.

Tolstoy, Leo. His last message to mankind, written for the 18th International Peace Congress held at Stockholm in 1909. http://www.jesusradicals.com/library/tolstoy/last.html.

War Dogs, America's Forgotten Heroes: The Untold Story of Dogs in Combat. Narrated by Martin Sheen. VHS. (GRB, Nature's Recipe Pet Foods, 1999

ABOUT THE AUTHOR

 Captain Paul K. Chappell graduated from West Point in 2002 and was deployed to Baghdad during 2006 and 2007. He now serves as the commander of a Patriot Battery at Fort Bliss, Texas. He is finishing his second book, *Peaceful Revolution*, which explains in detail how together we can end the wars between countries, our ongoing war with nature, and the suffering in our hearts. For more information on how we can make a difference, and to connect with others who want to build a brighter future, please go to www.paulkchappell.com.

AUTHOR'S NOTE

All my royalties from sales of this book will be donated to nonprofit organizations that support veterans of wars. For more information about organizations that will receive donations, please visit www.paulkchappell.com.

On the website, we will also maintain an ongoing list of organizations and other resources for the active promotion of peace.

Author's Family

Paul K. Chappell's father, First Sergeant Paul B. Chappell, during the Vietnam War.

Paul K. Chappell's mother, Mi-Suk Chappell, in Korea during the 1960s

Family Photo (1981)

Publisher's Note

Will War Ever End? is a book we felt must be published. Along with its accompanying website, we hope this book will contribute to meaningful change in the way people look at our world and how we live, not only with our fellow humans, but with our fellow beings of all kinds. Humans are violent not only to each other but to the natural world we inhabit. We have reached a point of no return in our relationships with each other and with our planet. Our commitment to helping make that change is the reason this book exists. Any profits that come to us from publishing this book will be dedicated to furthering its goals. When you buy a copy of *Will War Ever End?* you are making a contribution to help change the world.

RECOMMENDED RESOURCES

A Force More Powerful, DVD, A Force More Powerful Films, 2002

The Bonus Army: An American Epic, Paul Dickson and Thomas B. Allen, New York: Walker & Company, 2006

Bury the Chains: Prophets and Rebels in the Fight to Free an Empire's Slaves, Adam Hochschild, New York: Mariner Books, 2006

On Killing: The Psychological Cost of Learning to Kill in War and Society, Lt. Col. Dave Grossman, U.S. Army (ret), Boston: Back Bay Books, 1996

Soldiers of Conscience, DVD, Luna Productions, 2008

War Is a Racket: The Antiwar Classic by America's Most Decorated Soldier, Smedley D. Butler, Los Angeles: Feral House, 2003

Why We Fight, DVD, Sony Pictures, 2006